Grammar & Punctuation
Pupil Book Year 1

Rachel Axten-Higgs

Features of this book

- Clear explanations and worked examples for each grammar and punctuation topic from the KS1 National Curriculum.

- Questions split into three sections that become progressively more challenging:

Warm up

Test yourself

Challenge yourself

- 'How did you do?' checks at the end of each topic for self-evaluation.

- Regular progress tests to assess pupils' understanding and recap on their learning.

- Answers to every question in a pull-out section at the centre of the book.

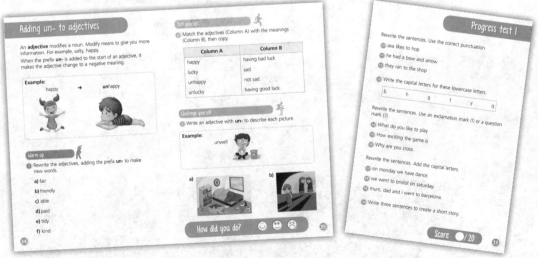

Contents

Forming sentences

A **sentence** is a group of words that work together to give the reader a whole thought.

> **Example:**
>
> I went to the zoo.

A **sentence** must make sense to the reader. It is important that the words are in the **correct order**, otherwise it is very confusing.

> **Example:**
>
> zoo went I the to.
> I went to the zoo. ✓

Warm up

1 Copy and complete the sentences using the words in the box.

books	happy	playing	red

a) I like _____ with my dad.

b) Caleb likes to read _____ .

c) I have a _____ dog.

d) I saw a _____ bus.

2 Rewrite the sentences. Put the words in the correct order so they make sense.

a) He a happy monkey is.

b) I like to play my friends with.

c) teddy I miss my.

d) I dance love to.

e) We roundabout went the on.

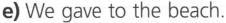

Challenge yourself

3 Find an incorrect word in each sentence. Then rewrite the sentences correctly.

a) We like eating films.

b) Sam hopes a dog called Ben.

c) It is fun to shop to music.

d) The game is fun to eat.

e) We gave to the beach.

How did you do?

Separating words with spaces

In your writing, you must leave **spaces between words** so that your reader knows where a word begins and ends.

This makes it easier for a reader to understand what you are writing.

It also makes it easier for you to read back through your writing to check it.

Example:

It is difficult to read this sentence without spaces between the words:

Icanseeadog.

It is much easier to read when there are spaces between the words:

I can see a dog.

 Warm up

1. Which of these sentences has got spaces in the correct places?

a) Iam Bob.

b) Iamfun.

c) Who am I?

2 Rewrite the sentences with spaces in the correct places.

a) Mymumiskind.

b) Irunveryfast.

c) Ilovetoplayfootball.

d) Iamhappytoday.

Challenge yourself

3 Write a complete sentence to answer each question. Remember to put a space between each word.

a) What colour is the hat?

b) What can you see?

c) How is the girl feeling?

How did you do?

Capital letters and full stops

At the beginning of a **sentence**, you need to write a **capital letter**.

Look at the capital letters in alphabetical order:

A B C D E F G H I J K L M N O P Q R S T U V W X Y Z

You have to use punctuation at the end of a **sentence** to show your reader that it is the end of that particular thought (sentence).

Most sentences end with a **full stop**.

Example:

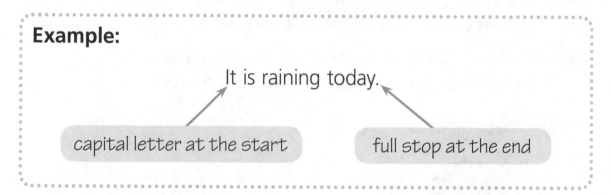

It is raining today.

capital letter at the start

full stop at the end

Warm up

① Rewrite the sentences using the correct punctuation and capital letters where necessary.

a) he went to the shop

b) we are going to school today

c) they like to dance

d) she is six today

2 Rewrite each sentence as two sentences. Use the correct punctuation and capital letters where necessary.

a) it is raining today we are going to get wet

b) we played in the park i like playing with my friends

c) i like playing football my friend likes playing cricket

d) maya is crying she hurt her leg

Challenge yourself

3 Rewrite the sentences. Put the words in the correct order and use the correct punctuation and capital letters where necessary.

a) beach went we to the

b) called Jamal i am

c) in park we the play

d) time it for is school

When you write a **sentence** that asks a **question**, you must end it with a **question mark (?)**.

The words **who**, **what**, **where**, **when**, **how** and **which** often start questions.

> **Examples:**
>
> **Who** is your best friend**?**
>
> **What** is your name**?**
>
> **Where** do you live**?**
>
> **When** will the cakes be ready**?**
>
> **How** many sisters do you have**?**
>
> **Which** way is your house**?**

If you want to show some **surprise**, then you use an **exclamation mark (!)**.

> **Examples:**
>
> How funny**!**
>
> What a silly face**!**

Warm up

1 Copy the sentences. Use a full stop (.) or a question mark (?) at the end.

a) How old are you

b) My name is Oscar

c) I like playing at the park

d) What is your name

e) Where is your mum

2 Rewrite the sentences. Use an exclamation mark (!) or a question mark (?).

a) What do you like playing

b) Why were you late for school

c) What big teeth you have, Grandma

d) What a lovely picnic Mummy has made

e) How loud that police siren is

Challenge yourself

3 Rewrite the sentences. Use an exclamation mark (!), a full stop (.) or a question mark (?).

a) It is sunny today

b) Where are the keys

c) How unusual to like spiders

d) Why are you sad

e) What a treat to have ice-cream

f) What day is it

How did you do?

Capital letters for names

When you write the **name** of a person or place, you use a **capital letter** at the beginning of the word.

These words are called **proper nouns**.

Examples:

Proper nouns are:

- people's names: *Shabana, Anoushka, Ted*
- places: *London, France, Catcott School*
- days, months, festivals:
  Tuesday, September, New Year's Day

When you write the **personal pronoun 'I'** you always use a capital letter.

Examples:

I went to the park.

My sister and **I** like doing ballet.

Warm up

1 Write answers to the questions. Use capital letters for proper nouns.

a) What's your name?

b) What's your friend's name?

c) Where do you live?

d) What day comes after Thursday?

e) What month comes before April?

2 Rewrite the sentences. Add the missing capital letters.

a) We went to school on monday.

b) Yesterday, i flew to edinburgh.

c) My name is eliza.

d) levi, ryan and raoul are friends.

e) It snowed in december.

Challenge yourself

3 Rewrite the passage. Fill the gaps with proper nouns and correct the **two** words that should have capital letters.

On _____ (day of the week), i went to

_____ (place).

I had lots of fun as i went with my friends _____

(friend 1) and _____ (friend 2).

How did you do?

Sequencing sentences

When you want to write a short story, you need to write **sentences** in the **correct order** so that it makes sense.

Example:

We played on the swings at the park. I fell off the swing. I hurt my arm.

Warm up

1 Choose the story which is in the correct order.

a) After tea, I built a sandcastle. We ate fish and chips for tea. We drove to the seaside.

b) We drove to the seaside. We ate fish and chips for tea. After tea, I built a sandcastle.

c) After tea, I built a sandcastle. We drove to the seaside. We ate fish and chips for tea.

2 Write the sentences in the correct order.

a) Mum picked me up from school. I ate my lunch at school. I went to school.

b) I ate my tea. Dad cooked my tea. I had a bath after tea.

c) We made a fire. We cooked marshmallows on the fire. We found some sticks to make a fire.

Challenge yourself

3 Write one more sentence to finish each short story.

a) I played in the garden. It started to rain.

_____ .

b) I made the body and head of a snowman. Then I put the

arms and buttons on. _____ .

c) Mum filled up the paddling pool. I put my swimming

costume on. _____ .

d) We arrived at the cinema. We sat in our seats.

_____ .

e) I made some bread. I put it in the oven to bake.

_____ .

How did you do?

Rewrite the sentences with spaces in the correct places.

1. Myteacheriskind.

2. Iplayinthepark.

3. Howoldareyou?

Rewrite the sentences. Put the words in the correct order.

4. is snowing It today.

5. are going When you park? the to

6. present Grandad gave me! big What a

Find an incorrect word in each sentence. Then rewrite the sentences so that they make sense.

7. We rolled to school.

8. The beach has grass on it.

9. We danced in the sea on holiday.

Rewrite the sentences. Use the correct punctuation.

10 ava likes to hop

11 he had a bow and arrow

12 they ran to the shop

13 Write the capital letters for these lowercase letters.

| b | h | g | t | y | q |

Rewrite the sentences. Use an exclamation mark (!) or a question mark (?).

14 What do you like to play

15 How exciting the game is

16 Why are you cross

Rewrite the sentences. Add the capital letters.

17 on monday we have dance.

18 we went to bristol on saturday.

19 mum, dad and i went to barcelona.

20 Write three sentences to create a short story.

Score ⬤ / 20   **17**

Using *and* in sentences

We can use **and** to join two sentences together or to add extra information to a sentence.

Examples:

I like playing football **and** I like swimming.

James ate his tea **and** then he went to bed.

Isaac kicked the ball **and** broke the window.

1 Copy and complete the sentences using the word 'and' and the words in the box.

| I opened the door | so does my friend | went on holiday |

a) I ran to the house _____.

b) We packed the car _____.

c) I like playing netball _____.

2 Match the beginnings of the sentences (Column A) with the ends (Column B). Then write complete sentences, using the word 'and' to join the two parts.

Column A	Column B
James went to the shops	ate her tea.
Ayumi ran home	swam in the sea.
I went to the seaside	bought a toy.

3 Copy each sentence and finish it with an extra piece of information. Use the word 'and' to connect the two ideas.

a) I like reading…

b) We went to the park…

c) I ate my dinner…

d) I like eating fruit…

How did you do?

Plural nouns 1

A **noun** is a word used to identify a person, place, animal or object, for example, lady, home, otter or chair.

A **singular noun** is used to identify a single item.

Examples:

one book, one egg, one chair

We use a **plural noun** when we are talking about more than one thing.

We add **-s** to most nouns to make them plural.

Examples:

two book**s**, eight egg**s**, 18 chair**s**

Warm up

1 Rewrite these singular nouns as plural nouns.

a) pen

b) table

c) coat

d) duck

2 Copy and write the plural nouns.

a) one cat / five _____

b) one boat / two _____

c) one car / seven _____

d) a goat / six _____

e) a plane / three _____

Challenge yourself

3 Copy and complete the sentences using the words in the box.

apples	cows	hat	hats	cow	apple

a) I saw lots of _____ sleeping in the field.

b) He wore a _____ on his head.

c) The farmer milked a _____ .

d) There were _____ on the tree.

e) He could not choose which of his _____ to wear that day.

f) There was a single _____ at the very top of the tree.

How did you do?

Plural nouns 2

We also sometimes use the ending **-es** to make plurals.
We use this when a **noun** ends in **s**, **z**, **x**, **ch** or **sh**.

Examples:

one glass, two glass**es**

a buzz, three buzz**es**

a box, six box**es**

a match, four match**es**

one bush, two bush**es**

Warm up

1 Rewrite the singular nouns as plural nouns.

a) scratch

b) lunch

c) wish

d) kiss

e) dash

f) fox

Answers

Pages 4–5

1.
   a) I like playing with my dad.
   b) Caleb likes to read books.
   c) I have a happy dog.
   d) I saw a red bus.
2.
   a) He is a happy monkey.
   b) I like to play with my friends.
   c) I miss my teddy.
   d) I love to dance.
   e) We went on the roundabout.
3. **Answers will vary, e.g.**
   a) We like watching films. / We like eating cake.
   b) Sam has a dog called Ben.
   c) It is fun to dance / sing to music.
   d) The game is fun to play.
   e) We went to the beach. / We gave to the charity.

Pages 6–7

1. c)
2.
   a) My mum is kind.
   b) I run very fast.
   c) I love to play football.
   d) I am happy today.
3. **Answers will vary, e.g.**
   a) The hat is red.
   b) I can see a boat.
   c) The girl is feeling sad / unhappy.

Pages 8–9

1.
   a) He went to the shop.
   b) We are going to school today.
   c) They like to dance.
   d) She is six today.
2.
   a) It is raining today. We are going to get wet. / It is raining. Today, we are going to get wet.
   b) We played in the park. I like playing with my friends.
   c) I like playing football. My friend likes playing cricket.
   d) Maya is crying. She hurt her leg.
3.
   a) We went to the beach.
   b) I am called Jamal.
   c) We play in the park.
   d) It is time for school.

Pages 10–11

1.
   a) How old are you?
   b) My name is Oscar.
   c) I like playing at the park.
   d) What is your name?
   e) Where is your mum?
2.
   a) What do you like playing?
   b) Why were you late for school?
   c) What big teeth you have, Grandma!
   d) What a lovely picnic Mummy has made!
   e) How loud that police siren is!
3.
   a) It is sunny today.
   b) Where are the keys?
   c) How unusual to like spiders!
   d) Why are you sad?
   e) What a treat to have ice-cream!
   f) What day is it?

Pages 12–13

1 a–c) **Answers will vary.**
   d) Friday
   e) March
2.
   a) We went to school on Monday.
   b) Yesterday, I flew to Edinburgh.
   c) My name is Eliza.
   d) Levi, Ryan and Raoul are friends.
   e) It snowed in December.
3. **Answers will vary, e.g.**
   On Wednesday, I went to London. I had lots of fun as I went with my friends Freya and Oscar.

Pages 14–15

1. b)
2.
   a) I went to school. I ate my lunch at school. Mum picked me up from school.
   b) Dad cooked my tea. I ate my tea. I had a bath after tea.
   c) We found some sticks to make a fire. We made a fire. We cooked marshmallows on the fire.
3. **Answers will vary, e.g.**
   a) I came inside.
   b) Then I put the face on.
   c) I got in the paddling pool.
   d) The film started. / We watched the film.
   e) I took it out of the oven.

Answers

1. My teacher is kind.
2. I play in the park.
3. How old are you?
4. It is snowing today.
5. When are you going to the park?
6. What a big present Grandad gave me!
7. **Answers will vary, e.g.**
   We walked to school.
8. **Answers will vary, e.g.**
   The beach has sand on it.
9. **Answers will vary, e.g.**
   We swam in the sea on holiday.
10. Ava likes to hop.
11. He had a bow and arrow.
12. They ran to the shop.
13. B, H, G, T, Y, Q
14. What do you like to play?
15. How exciting the game is!
16. Why are you cross?
17. On Monday we have dance.
18. We went to Bristol on Saturday.
19. Mum, Dad and I went to Barcelona.
20. **Answers will vary.**

Pages 18–19

1. a) I ran to the house and I opened the door.
   b) We packed the car and went on holiday.
   c) I like playing netball and so does my friend.
2. James went to the shops and bought a toy.
   Ayumi ran home and ate her tea.
   I went to the seaside and swam in the sea.
3. **Answers will vary.**

Pages 20–21

1. a) pens
   b) tables
   c) coats
   d) ducks
2. a) five cats
   b) two boats
   c) seven cars
   d) six goats
   e) three planes
3. a) I saw lots of cows sleeping in the field.
   b) He wore a hat on his head.
   c) The farmer milked a cow.
   d) There were apples on the tree.
   e) He could not choose which of his hats to wear that day.
   f) There was a single apple at the very top of the tree.

Pages 22–23

1. a) scratches
   b) lunches
   c) wishes
   d) kisses
   e) dashes
   f) foxes
2. a) coaches
   b) dishes
   c) crowns
   d) boxes
   e) pianos
3. a) three girls
   b) five brushes
   c) a few houses
   d) three watches
   e) four bosses

Pages 24–25

1. a) S
   b) S
   c) P
   d) P
   e) S
2. dog – a pet that barks
   dogs – pets that bark
   tap – water comes out of this
   taps – water comes out of these
   brush – we use this to sweep the floor
   brushes – we use these to sweep floors
3. a) carpets
   b) cats
   c) lunch
   d) boy
   e) dog

Pages 26–27

1. a) walking
   b) shouting
   c) watching
   d) talking
2. a) thinks, thinking
   b) winks, winking
   c) plants, planting
   d) sings, singing
3. a) Amira walks to school.
   b) We were throwing the ball to each other.
   c) Mrs Tims was shouting at the boy.
   d) Freya likes watching plays.
   e) Daniel always smiles at people when they talk to him.

Answers

Pages 28–29
1. a) teacher
   b) walker
   c) reader
   d) talker
2. a) designed, designer
   b) called, caller
   c) kicked, kicker
   d) jumped, jumper
3. a) The painter painted a lovely picture of a sunflower.
   b) The cleaner is tired today. He cleaned the whole school yesterday.

Pages 30–31
1. **Answers will vary, e.g.** I went to the shop and bought sweets.
2. **Answers will vary, e.g.** I play football and my friend plays too.
3. S
4. P
5. P
6. foxes
7. pears
8. matches
9. cup
10. watch
11. wish
12. jump(ing)
13. throw(er)
14. help(s)
15. He shouted for help.
16. I was the best helper today.
17. The boat was sinking.
One of the following:
18. kicks, kicking, kicked, kicker
19. reads, reading, reader
20. sings, singing, singer

Pages 32–33
1. a) unlock
   b) undress
   c) unhook
   d) uncover
   e) unfold
2. a) I had to unzip the zip on my coat to take it off.
   b) Mina had to untie her laces.
   c) They had to undo their mistake.
   d) Pat had to unpack his bag.
3. a) unbutton / undo
   b) unload / unpack
   c) unpack

Pages 34–35
1. a) unfair
   b) unfriendly
   c) unable
   d) unpaid
   e) untidy
   f) unkind
2. happy = not sad
   lucky = having good luck
   unhappy = sad
   unlucky = having bad luck
3. a) untidy
   b) unkind / unfriendly / unhappy

Pages 36–37
1. a) I did my work quickly.
   b) I wasn't doing anything.
   c) If you were older, you could watch that film.
   d) I am not going to walk to school.
2. a) I <u>did</u> it because I had to.
   b) I <u>am not</u> going to help because it is boring.
   c) Kenzo used <u>those</u> pens for his work.
3. a) We <u>done</u> lots of walking. (did)
   b) We ate <u>them</u> pears for snack. (those)
   c) I didn't wear my coat cos it <u>weren't</u> cold. (wasn't)
   d) Leon <u>ain't</u> going to the park. (isn't)

Pages 38–39
1. a) Please stop talking!
   b) My name is Amari.
   c) How old are you?
   d) The dog is running away.
   e) I am going to Paris.
2. **Answers will vary as children may choose to correct either the amounts or the nouns.**
   a) Incorrect. I have three cats.
   b) Correct.
   c) Incorrect. Oscar has one sister.
   d) Incorrect. We have six dogs.
   e) Correct.
   f) Incorrect. We went on two buses.
3. I went to school because it was Tuesday. I forgot to take my PE kit. I did PE in a school kit. I will bring my kit next week.

Answers

Pages 40–41

1.
   a) Please can you help me?
   b) I have three rats.
   c) Jack did the work.
   d) What a horrible boy he is!

2. **Answers will vary, e.g.**
   It was a cold, wet day outside. Beth sat on the windowsill above the radiator. She was glad she was indoors. She fell asleep. She had a dream that she was on a boat and the sea was all around her. Suddenly she woke up. Water was dripping onto her head.

3. **Children's own discussion.**

Pages 42–43

1. Mum says my room is untidy.
2. I had to untie my laces.
3. It makes me unhappy when my friend is sad.
4. **Answers will vary.**
5. unfair = not treating people the same
6. unable = not able to do something
7. unfriendly = not being nice to other people
8. unpaid = not being given money for doing something
9. Jay did it.
10. It was because/cos I had to.
11. I am not going to help.
12. What a lovely day we've had!
13. Do you like toys?
14. I am called Tim.
15–20. I like playing / to play in puddles. I wear boots. They are shiny boots. I jump very high so the water splashes lots.

2 Copy the correct spelling of each plural noun.

a) coachs / coaches

b) dishs / dishes

c) crowns / crownes

d) boxs / boxes

e) pianos / pianoes

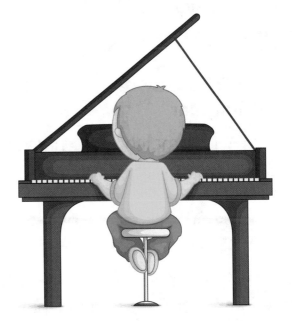

Challenge yourself

3 Copy and write the plural nouns by adding **-s** or **-es** to the singular nouns.

a) one girl / three _____

b) a brush / five _____

c) a house / a few _____

d) one watch / three _____

e) one boss / four _____

How did you do?

More plurals

When **-s** or **-es** is added to a **noun**, the noun changes from **singular** to **plural**.

Examples:

Singular	Plural
match = one match	matches = more than one match
horse = one horse	horses = more than one horse

Sometimes there is a number before the noun that tells us if it is singular or plural.

Examples: **one** jug   **three** jug**s**

Sometimes there are other words that tell us if the noun is singular or plural.

Examples:

Singular	Plural
This cat	**These** cat**s**
A dish	**Lots of** dish**es**

Warm up

1. Copy the nouns and write (S) for singular or (P) for plural.

a) game   **b)** mouse   **c)** drinks

d) wishes   **e)** cup

2 Match the singular and plural nouns (Column A) with the meanings (Column B). Use the words in bold to help you decide if the meaning refers to a singular or a plural noun.

Column A	Column B
dog	water comes out of **this**
dogs	**a** pet that barks
tap	water comes out of **these**
taps	we use **this** to sweep the floor
brush	we use **these** to sweep floors
brushes	**pets** that bark

3 Write the correct version of the noun in brackets to complete each sentence.

a) There were lots of (carpet) to choose from in the shop.

b) When my Mum was a girl she had ten (cat).

c) I had a hot school (lunch) today.

d) This (boy) is very clever.

e) We took a (dog) for a walk.

How did you do?

Adding -s and -ing to verbs

Verbs are 'doing' words, e.g. run, skip, throw.

We can add letters to the ends of **verbs** as well as **nouns**. These are called **suffixes**, for example, **-s** and **-ing**.

> **Examples:**
>
> play → play**s**, play**ing**
> throw → throw**s**, throw**ing**

We add **-s** to verbs when we talk about something that he, she or it often does.

> **Examples:**
>
> He play**s** in the snow every winter.
> The cat often sit**s** in the sunshine.

We add **-ing** to verbs when we talk about something that we are doing now or we were doing in the past. Also, we use the **-ing** form after some verbs, for example 'like'.

> **Examples:**
>
> I am play**ing** in the snow at the moment.
> We were eat**ing** our lunch at one o'clock yesterday.
> They like play**ing** football.

Warm up

1 Copy the verbs, adding **-ing** to make new words.

a) walk   **b)** shout   **c)** watch   **d)** talk

2 Copy the verbs, adding **-s** and **-ing** to make new words.

> **Example:**
>
> stand ➜ stand**s** stand**ing**

a) think

b) wink

c) plant

d) sing

Challenge yourself

3 Copy and complete the sentences using the words in the box.

| watching | walks | throwing | shouting | smiles |

a) Amira _____ to school.

b) We were _____ the ball to each other.

c) Mrs Tims was _____ at the boy.

d) Freya likes _____ plays.

e) Daniel always _____ at people when they talk to him.

How did you do?

Adding -ed and -er to verbs

As well as **-s** and **-ing**, we can also add other suffixes like **-ed** and **-er** to **verbs**.

> **Examples:**
>
> help ➜ helps, helping, help**ed**, help**er**
>
> work ➜ works, working, work**ed**, work**er**

We add **-ed** to a verb when we are talking about something that happened in the past.

> **Example:**
>
> We play**ed** football yesterday.

We add **-er** to a verb when we are talking about the person who does the action.

> **Example:**
>
> The football play**er** scored a goal.

Warm up

1 Copy the verbs, adding **-er** to make new words.

a) teach

b) walk

c) read

d) talk

2 Copy the verbs, adding **-ed** and **-er** to make new words.

> **Example:**
>
> help ➔ help**ed**   help**er**

a) design

b) call

c) kick

d) jump

Challenge yourself

3 Copy and complete the sentences using the word given and the endings **-er** and **-ed**.

> paint

a) The _____ _____ a lovely picture of a sunflower.

> clean

b) The _____ is tired today. He _____ the whole school yesterday.

How did you do?

Progress test 2

Finish each sentence by adding extra information using the word 'and'.

1 I went to the shop…

2 I play football…

Write (S) if the noun is singular and (P) if the noun is plural.

3 garden

4 swings

5 hutches

Write these singular nouns as plural nouns.

6 fox

7 pear

8 match

Write these plural nouns as singular nouns.

9 cups

10 watches

11 wishes

Copy the verbs and circle the endings that have been added.

12 jumping

13 thrower

14 helps

Copy and complete the sentences using the words in the box.

sinking	shouted	helper

15 He _____ for help.

16 I was the best _____ today.

17 The boat was _____.

Add letters to each verb to form a new word.

18 kick

19 read

20 sing

Score ⬤ / 20   **31**

Adding *un-* to verbs

When the prefix **un-** is added to the start of a **verb**, it makes the verb change to a negative meaning.

Example:

tie = do something up

untie = undo something

 Warm up

1 Rewrite the verbs, adding the prefix **un-** to make new words.

a) lock

b) dress

c) hook

d) cover

e) fold

2 Copy and complete the sentences using the words in the box.

untie	unpack	unzip	undo

a) I had to _____ the zip on my coat to take it off.

b) Mina had to _____ her laces.

c) They had to _____ their mistake.

d) Pat had to _____ his bag.

Challenge yourself

3 Write a verb with **un-** to describe each picture.

Example:

unzip

a)

b)

c)

How did you do?

Adding *un-* to adjectives

An **adjective** modifies a noun. Modify means to give you more information. For example, salty, happy.

When the prefix **un-** is added to the start of an adjective, it makes the adjective change to a negative meaning.

Example:

happy   →   **un**happy

 Warm up

1 Rewrite the adjectives, adding the prefix **un-** to make new words.

a) fair

b) friendly

c) able

d) paid

e) tidy

f) kind

2 Match the adjectives (Column A) with the meanings (Column B), then copy.

Column A	Column B
happy	having bad luck
lucky	sad
unhappy	not sad
unlucky	having good luck

Challenge yourself

3 Write an adjective with **un-** to describe each picture.

Example:

unwell

a)

b)

How did you do?

Standard English

Standard English is when you write and speak using the English language properly.

> **Example:**
>
> I did it because I was asked to. (STANDARD ENGLISH)
>
> I done it cos I were asked to. (NON-STANDARD ENGLISH)

Warm up

1 Which of the sentences are written in Standard English? Copy the correct sentence from each pair.

a) I done my work quickly.
   I did my work quickly.

b) I wasn't doing anything.
   I wasn't doing nothing.

c) If you was older, you could watch that film.
   If you were older, you could watch that film.

d) I am not going to walk to school.
   I ain't gonna walk to school.

2 Rewrite the sentences in Standard English. Replace the underlined words with the words in the box.

am not	did	those

a) I <u>done</u> it because I had to.

b) I <u>ain't</u> going to help because it's boring.

c) Kenzo used <u>them</u> pens for his work.

3 Copy the sentences and underline the words that are Non-standard English. Can you write these words in Standard English?

a) We done lots of walking.

b) We ate them pears for snack.

c) I didn't wear my coat cos it weren't cold.

d) Leon ain't going to the park.

How did you do?

Talking about writing 1

When you finish a piece of writing, it is important you read it to yourself to check you have written what you meant to write.

When you read, look out for:

- PUNCTUATION – full stops, capital letters, question marks, exclamation marks. Have you used them in the right places? Have you missed any?

- WORDS – have you used plural words when you mean more than one thing? Have you added the suffixes **-s** or **-es** to plural nouns?

- SENTENCES – have you written your words in sentences? Do your sentences start and end correctly? Are the sentences in the right order?

- SPELLING – have you spelled your words correctly?

Warm up

1 Rewrite the sentences correctly.

a) please stop talking.

b) my name is amari.

c) how old are you!

d) the dog is running away.

e) i am going to paris?

2 Are the sentences correct or incorrect? Rewrite any sentences that are incorrect.

a) I have three cat.

b) We have lots of pets.

c) Oscar has one sisters.

d) We have six dog.

e) I planted an apple pip in a pot.

f) We went on two bus.

3 Rewrite this passage correctly. Remember to make sure the sentences are in the correct order.

I forgot to take my PE kit? I went to school cos it was tuesday. I done PE in a school kit. I will brings my kit next week

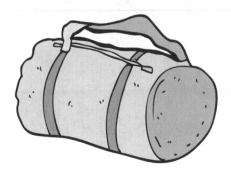

How did you do?

Talking about writing 2

When you have checked your own writing, it is a good idea to ask a friend to read it. They can help you check it and you can check their work too.

When you talk to your friend about their writing, try to use these words so that you are thinking about the important parts of the writing:

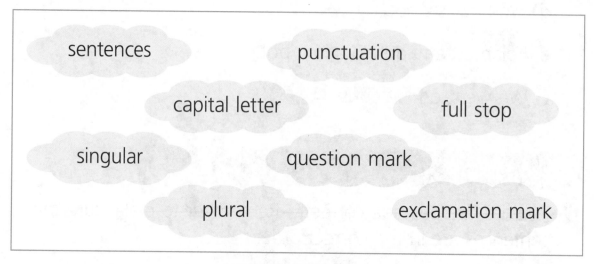

sentences

punctuation

capital letter

full stop

singular

question mark

plural

exclamation mark

1 Rewrite the sentences correctly. Then check your answers with a partner.

a) please can you help me.

b) i have three rat.

c) jack done the work

d) what a horrible boy he is

2 Read this passage with a partner. Then talk about the mistakes:

- Did you both find all the mistakes?

- Did you like the piece of writing? Why / Why not?

> It was a cold, wet days outside? beth sat on the windowsill above the radiator. she was glad she was indoors She fell asleep? she had a dream that she was on a boats and the sea was all around her. Suddenly she woke up. water was drippingontoherhead.

Challenge yourself

3 Work with a partner. Read a short piece of their writing. Tell them two things you like about it and one thing they could do better. Use some of the words from the box on page 40.

How did you do?

Progress test 3

Copy and complete the sentences using the words in the box.

untie	untidy	unhappy

1 Mum says my room is _____ .

2 I had to _____ my laces.

3 It makes me _____ when my friend is sad.

4 Write a sentence using this word.

  unpack

5 – **8** Match the words (Column A) with the meanings (Column B), then copy.

Column A	Column B
unfair	not being nice to other people
unable	not treating people the same
unfriendly	not being given money for doing something
unpaid	not able to do something

Rewrite the sentences in Standard English.

9 Jay done it.

10 It were cos I had to.

11 I ain't going to help.

Rewrite the sentences correctly.

12 what a lovely day we've had

13 do you like toys

14 i am called tim

15 – **20** Find **six** mistakes in the passage and rewrite it correctly.

> I like play in puddles. I wear boot. They are shiny boots i jump
> very high so the water splash lots

Published by Keen Kite Books
An imprint of HarperCollins*Publishers* Ltd
The News Building
1 London Bridge Street
London SE1 9GF

ISBN 9780008184506

First published in 2016

10 9 8 7 6 5 4 3 2 1

Text and design © 2016 Keen Kite Books, an imprint of HarperCollins*Publishers* Ltd

Author: Rachel Axten-Higgs

Series Concept and Commissioning: Michelle I'Anson
Series Editor and Development: Shelley Teasdale & Fiona Watson
Inside Concept Design: Paul Oates
Project Manager: Rebecca Adlard
Cover Design: Anthony Godber
Text Design and Layout: Q2A Media
Production: Lyndsey Rogers
Printed in the UK

A CIP record of this book is available from the British Library.

Images are ©Shutterstock.com